THE MOUTH

The Mouth of Earth

POEMS

Sarah P. Strong

UNIVERSITY OF NEVADA PRESS | *Reno & Las Vegas*

University of Nevada Press, Reno, Nevada 89557 USA
www.unpress.nevada.edu

Copyright © 2020 by University of Nevada Press

LIBRARY OF CONGRESS CATALOGING-IN-PUBLICATION DATA
Names: Strong, Sarah Pemberton, 1967– author.
Title: The mouth of earth : poems / Sarah P. Strong.
Description: Reno ; Las Vegas : University of Nevada Press, [2020] |
Summary: "Poems in The Mouth of Earth contemplate how we might live wisely in
  the midst of a planetary change we barely comprehend. The book is a contribution to
  21st century environmental literature, and a survival guide to the planet and one another
  in the age of climate crisis"—Provided by publisher.
Identifiers: LCCN 2020017802 (print) | LCCN 2020017803 (ebook) |
  ISBN 9781948908849 (paperback) | ISBN 9781948908856 (ebook)
Subjects: LCGFT: Poetry.
Classification: LCC PS3619.T78 M68 2020 (print) | LCC PS3619.T78 (ebook) |
  DDC 811/.6—dc23
LC record available at https://lccn.loc.gov/2020017802
LC ebook record available at https://lccn.loc.gov/2020017803

The paper used in this book is a recycled stock made from 30 percent post-consumer waste
materials, certified by FSC, and meets the requirements of American National Standard
for Information Sciences—Permanence of Paper for Printed Library Materials, ANSI/NISO
Z39.48-1992 (R2002). Binding materials were selected for strength and durability.

FIRST PRINTING

Manufactured in the United States of America

24 23 22 21 20   5 4 3 2 1

For Vee and Cecilia

Contents

III.

~ I ~

Fire Burns Grass

On the third day of the wildfire she answers.
I press the ancient phone receiver to my head.
This phone—so old I think I'm talking
to the dead sometimes. *Talk to me. Talk to me.*

She says, *Remember when we changed the game?*

Three fingers at her lips meant water.
My hand upturned, half-opened, stood for grass.
Her fist, bursting into fingers, meant flames.

Yes—talk to me.

The phone at my face like an oxygen mask.

But not the rules. We kept the rules the same.

(grass drinks water)
(water puts out fire)
(fire burns grass)

Will you have to leave your house?

She laughs at that. Her laugh: a match struck
in a rainstorm, impossible spark

of old longing inside me.
Outside my window,

the springtime is coming apart;
sheets of rain
clog the sewer with drowned cherry blossoms.

Are you still there?

I'm thirsty but I can't reach the sink,
the phone's umbilicus is already stretched taut. Outside,
a gust of wind tears a branch from the dogwood.

Oh, yes. Rooted to my spot.

Mobile

It seems it's not enough for us
to love the earth the way we loved, as infants,
a milky nipple. What the teacher meant

when he told his students, *Carry water in a sieve!*
No one could until, at cliff's edge, he showed them—
flung the metal basket into the Pacific.

But we don't sink into the world like that.
We rise up from the earth's breast
and crane our necks over the grasses, distracted

by a glimpse of shiny things. You can see it
in the baby by eight months:
she'll be nursing along in the garden of contentment

until some glint of motion snags her eye,
and the world not even named yet—
that blur of green is not yet

"flock of wild parakeets in northern coastal city,"
the pink flash not yet classified
as "musical mobile of plastic ponies,"

a baby shower gift I could not bring myself to keep:
the music box rendered "The Blue Danube Waltz"
as a series of electronic beeps

while the ponies rotated, trailing a squishy plastic smell
that reminded me variously of asthma attacks,
factory workers in China, and Barbie dolls.

I saw the real Blue Danube once,
muddy with rain in Vienna, a river
whose headwaters start before the Roman Empire

and run through two world wars,
bearing fascism and Freudian psychology
and schnitzel all downriver to pour into the Black Sea

of our seemingly endless need to keep playing with matches.
To see what will catch light. I've heard
the real "Blue Danube" too—

once, from a man sitting alone on the edge
of the stage that was the twentieth century,
plucking the notes of the waltz on a classical guitar

with such exquisite tension between the sweeping music
of the river and the tiny syncopated pattern
of dancing feet that at least one person

in the sparse and hurried lunch-hour audience
put down her cell phone and wept.
Magpies like shiny objects too. As do

starlings, blue jays, crows. Perhaps the commonality
persists in us like our desire for flight, the way
a line of music can persist

until someone fashions the memory
of a time those notes flooded the banks of our feelings
with a mechanical ghost of itself

that plays us at our plastic worst. When what we wanted
was the green breath of those first fields,
blown toward us by the moving shapes of horses.

Border

Things different over there
the words for them different
the things themselves

all the same

she put her flesh
in the mouth of a coyote
so that he would take her

a cross

to mark the place
where someone
died trying

two white sticks

the ghost of cactus
and the clouds
back and forth

over our heads

an edge of thinking
beyond which we don't go
to save face

which is burning

the other country so close
one good arm
could break a window

On the Road to California

The eye thirsts for rest, the blood for salt, the tongue
for fresh water. From inside a container of night
that has lasted for months, the mouths of the honeybees
open still, sucking at nothing. Deep in their wax catacombs,
legs curl in, thin and pollenless. Mites drink
the fluids from their bodies, bound
for the Fresno almond orchards.

On Interstate 10 beyond Las Cruces,
the driver, who hasn't slept since Tuesday,
dozes off. The trailer jackknifes sideways,
drags along the asphalt, sends sparks
into the darkness as its top peels back
like a sardine can. The wooden hive boxes sail out
and smash. Trickles of sugar water,
meant to keep the colonies alive
during their winter in the truck,
leak out like gasoline.

Starving bees crawl from the splintered boxes,
rise in clots above the twisted metal.
When the engine catches fire and explodes,
they swarm. Later that night
two men and three women crossing the desert
look up. A black cloud's tremble
cancels out the moon.

> *Where are the almond trees' acres of bride lace?*
> > *Draped with a veil of poison to save us.*
>
> *What do we call this snake of a river?*
> > *A shoelace yanked out of a shoe.*
>
> *What is this fire that burns us to motion?*
> > *A compass whose needle is spinning.*
>
> *And the darkness?*
> > *Hums to itself.*

Phone Call After a Fire

"Listen," she says. "They opened up the road.
I get to drive home, finally, though
I shouldn't call it that—home—since
the house is gone. But on the other hand
it wasn't just the house I loved." She speaks
so fast I start to pace, back and forth
across my kitchen floor, as if to keep
abreast of her voice: "Of course it wasn't just
the house, it was the trees across the road,
the edge of desert giving way to pines,
the homes near mine, a neighborhood.
And did I mention," she says, "I've taken up
smoking again? It's my way of communing
with all the smoldering trees." She laughs.
It's there, the old drag in her throat. An ache
in mine. A *No* inside me—her lopsided house,
her grandma's rug. The guitar she never plays.
Her plants. The rocking chair her father built.
"Who said," she asks, "that this, any of this,
was ours?" Her laugh becomes a cough.
"And by the way, I've decided: when I die
I don't want to be buried: burned
is where it's at. Anyway, I have to go.
I want to try to find Rascal, at least.
He got out right before the firewall
was breached; I couldn't find him when
they dragged me out. Typical man, eh?"
I hear her lighter scratch. Then the long
drag of her inhale, during which I hold
my breath too, listening. For what?
Wind in the burnt matchsticks of trees,
or her cat, or the ghost of her cat.

Stalin

is the title of a book,
over seven hundred pages,
two inches thick in paperback,
that I read every word of,
taking notes. I got the only A in the class,
the professor told me later.

Thirty years have passed,
and what I remember now
is that Trotsky was killed with an ice axe
at his desk in Mexico.
Of the twenty million people who died under Joseph Stalin,
I know the manner and location of just one.
Which leaves a lot

of bare feet slowly freezing
on frozen ground, starvation, bodies
unaccounted for except by the meaninglessness
of a number whose actual representation of anything
is as beyond me as the hundreds of thousands

of words I once read about Stalin.
While I'm thinking this, two naked three-year-olds
run shrieking past. Watching the bright flash
of their limbs in watery motion,

the peeled stream of their bodies
pouring through the living room
of this house where there is no indication
there will ever be a midnight

knock on the front door, it strikes me:
two hundred or two hundred thousand
years ago, a naked child's body playing
looked as it does now—bursting and waving
like a field when all the crops are ripe,
and also humble, a seeker of humble things:

warmth, something to drink
when thirsty, tenderness—
and softly incapable of planning harm.

Turning On the Lights

When the sun goes down, the music starts up.
First clear single notes

of fireflies hover just above
the ground, then rise to the crowns

of trees; next, the distant tunings
of an orchestra of stars.

Then torches, gas jets turned with a key,
and in a flicker that leaps the chasm

between the nineteenth and twentieth centuries,
electricity. Each stringed filament

plucks a step on the path westward
as the music runs after the sunset,

chasing the sun. One by one, the cities of Earth join in
until the music can be known

from space, like the Great Wall of China.
Below the Wall, a small girl walks humming to herself.

Gray jacket, red plastic barrette.
She's going to the neighbor's

to fetch oil for the lamp. She walks quickly.
Her mother has told her to be home by dark.

Study Guide

How is ice converted to water?

The speed at which it occurs.

How is matter converted to energy?

A live penguin.

How are unbelievers converted to belief?

Through the application of heat.

Define *permanent.*

Some kind of wave.

What is the "date of last frost"?

Direct personal experience.

What does she want for her birthday?

The last straw.

Define *migration.*

A drop in the bucket.

Where is Western Antarctica?

Through the loss of mass.

Will this be on the final?

It fluctuates based on your location

Notes from Detroit

(at the Dutch Golden Age exhibit at the DIA)

Still Life with Fruit and Dead Hare

sheen of light on pewter pitcher
the rabbit nailed to the wall

ripe fig split open
cantaloupe encrusted with fibrous webs

live parakeets bombard the apricots

Bouquet of Flowers

wasps on the peonies
translucent spider

a butterfly attacks
the iron scent of the scattered carnations

the flowers at the edge
swallowed in darkness

Flowers in a Glass Vase

red poppies dusted black
with their own pollen

can you catch the scent of roses asks the placard
and suddenly

yes the air grows
sweet and slightly rotten

Preparation for a Meal

slimed innards of game bird
iridescent as any halo

hook run through the pheasant's skinned neck
the heart muscle stippled with white lobes of fat

pile of imported citrus symbolizing affluence
orange slices crusting over in the air
seeds drying out

shucked oysters leaking
translucent ooze

a snail hikes up the velvet

the wine half-drunk
the dark archway beyond

the heavy gilt frame holding it all in

Still Life with Fruits, Vegetables, and Dead Game

a pile of tanagers bones thin as leaf stems
flesh hardly a mouthful

silvered stalks of artichoke
deer with a broken neck

the only live creature in the painting
a bright red parrot perched atop the plums

its opaque eye fixed not on the fruit but us
blackened mouth opening

as if to speak

Diner

Our special today is pancakes served with maple-flavored corn syrup and decorated with maraschino cherries and pineapple rings, which we can arrange into the shape of a smiley face if you would like that.

I'll have the eggs.

Today we also have the blueberry blintzes, which come rolled up on a plate like little dolls in blankets the way you wish your mother used to make them but never did because she was always too hung-over on Saturday mornings to get out of bed and your dad had moved to another state.

Just the eggs, please.

Or perhaps you'd like the dieter's special: fruit cocktail and a scoop of low-fat cottage cheese, whose scientific relationship to weight loss is nonexistent, but eating it might make you feel virtuous and in control.

Bring me the eggs already, yes, yes, battery cages, beaks sawed off, and a cup of coffee, I know, endangered species' habitats wrecked by my daily addiction to caffeine. Or, never mind the coffee—I'll take a glass of water.

Our water has been treated for your dining safety with fluoride and chlorine to protect you from dysentery. Would you like ice and a straw?

I feel a bit sick, actually. I'll just have some dry toast.

Perhaps you would like my Purelled hand laid on your clammy forehead.

What I would like is the very tip of your tongue held against my closed lips until our bodies become the same temperature.

I could also crawl across this table and let you peel me out of this cheap polyester uniform without any reference to the ensuing tableau's visual likeness to last month's photo-spread in *Hustler*.

Could I get that with a paper napkin blindfold and a side of skin sticking to melamine?

Yes, but it's extra.

In that case I'll just have the toast, but with a pat of butter soaking through its gold aluminum wrapper like the sun going down over a major metropolitan city in America.

I'll bring you the check, folded into a white origami crane.

Deus ex Machina

I am opening a ceiling
so the lost water can come down.
It's lost its way among
the insulation and the lathe,

soaking downward through the joists,
sideways through the ceiling plaster.
The husband's looking up at me,
telling me how next year he'll be

on sabbatical in France.
The wife says, Don't
I get a say in this?
I cut the hole, and the wet heavens

fall in clods between them.
Now it is raining on their parquet,
raining through the dropcloth.
I ease the cracked drainpipe

down from the ceiling. The air
starts to smell faintly of shit.
"You're good at this," the husband flirts.
Jesus, says the wife's expression,

though she only shakes her head
a little bit. No pictures on these walls—
their huge house echoes
as if they'd already

moved out. Up on the ladder I realize
I'm near tears. I pretend
I'm a god in a play—I am going to make it
work out in the end; I have the tools

this time. Outside the window,
a whirlwind of dead leaves,
which the god takes
for butterflies.

Poolside

That summer all the kids were singing
of the land turned to ice.
Frozen, its princesses
sisters slim and white,
their huge eyes pools of snow.
The children's voices splitting through
the wet drug of that August—
early evening, yet even in the long shadow
of the trees by the water,
the heat held, shimmered,
held. And still the girls twirled for each other,
threw up their hands, cried out
to whomever might be listening
I don't care and *Let it go* and
Let the storm rage on.

The Apollos

If all twelve went back again
to stand where they could see

this small sphere we call home
rising blue and gray and distantly

warm, small as a raindrop
tongued from a lover's face,

and with that long view
of the cloudy, indistinct, and lovely shapes

suffering assumes
when seen from a distance,

how would these tiny props—vanished rivers,
cracked reactors, bullets, cops,

cathedrals in piles of gray stones,
our rising wisps of smoke,

our lead-leached bones—appear?
Looking down like that, could one

feel a shift inside his chest?
Could he—blessed with no

particular divinity—become
by virtue of this gaze alone

some sort of god? Albeit a human one
who doesn't really know

the fullness of his powers
or their limits, save that he can't

be everywhere at once,
and that he can only see at most

the lit side of a face,
and that if we don't weight him down, he floats—

At the End of Brooklyn

Winter, still. Through clouds,
a bright gray shimmer:

small, struggling sun.
Signs for the Cyclone

before the actual Cyclone.
Wonder Wheel,

not turning. Stopped rides
whiten in the wind,

skeletons dinosaurs
above the tar.

A scratched plaque tells
how many thousand

pounds of Bethlehem
steel built it all.

Waves break
the boardwalk,

slap of the Atlantic going on
without us

gulls taking the pier

and the air full of cries—

A Story

On the street of my childhood
a boy kept a pet boa constrictor.

The boa ate live mice, one per month.
The boy left home and left his mother

in charge of the feedings.
The mother, unaware

the boa had just eaten, dropped a second mouse
into the glass terrarium.

The boa was already full and not interested.
The mouse huddled in a corner, terrified.

After several days the mouse began to starve.
No mouse food in the terrarium.

The mother, unhappy in her role
as procurer for a snake,

kept as far away from the terrarium as possible
and did not notice

anything. Eventually
hunger grew stronger than terror

and the mouse
took a bite of the boa constrictor.

I won't prolong this.
The bite became infected and the boa died.

Eventually the mother noticed.
When the son came back

he found the palatial glass cage
inhabited by a single mouse.

When I think about this story now,
I think most often of all the life I've spent

being the huddled mouse,
in such danger, I felt,

but not.
It is harder to see I have also been the snake.

And the mother. Too many times
the mother.

But today when I thought of it,
I was the boy,

staring in amazement at a life
I would not have thought possible

had I not been there to witness firsthand
the blindness of the body

and the persistence of the body
and the circumstances

of the body among others,
the body that needs and needs

and forgets absolutely nothing.

~II~

Dust

Buffalo Grass

Light catches it in sway, blown into waves
by miles of wind crossing the earth,
shaping the earth until the plains extend

from what will someday be called Canada
to what will then be known as Texas.

The hooves of buffalo, the mouths of buffalo,
the thunderheads of buffalo gather, drifting

as they graze. The grasses' roots
reach deep into the earth, holding the plains
in place against the plains winds.

No word *plains*. No word *winds*. No *wheat*.

Hattie Clemons, farmer

Word came from Washington, they opened up
the part called No Man's Land. And we went in.
Anyone willing to try his hand
could get himself three hundred twenty acres.

I was twelve then. My family,
each family like ours, we just wanted
our own place. Anyone can understand that.
The land office said if we removed the prairie

grasses, more rain would reach the soil.
And that the weather had changed
for good—the droughts were past.

It was a sight, those big ploughs slicing up the sod
just like we'd slice a loaf of bread. The soil so rich
it looked like something we could eat.

Virgil T. Payne, veteran and farmer

I got home back in 'eighteen. Lucky—
alive, discharged, and with both legs,
both arms. Pa got a tractor that was like
a dozen horses with six ploughs.

Six hundred acres, wheat, all ours. We sold it
to those poor souls overseas, men
I'd met, maybe, in Germany or France.
They were starving over there. Here,

we got a good price. I gave my wife
a real house, our four girls anything
they liked. All I wanted
was dreams with no mud in them. Dreams

that didn't wake me in the night,
my body drenched in sweat, my throat in dust.

Eliza Barnett, farmer

We've had dust storms before,
of course, but not like these. Never
such darkness, or so thick. John says

just keep on tilling soil—rain follows
the plough, everyone knows. In town they say

that if the Indians before us did all right
here, so will we. When I lost
the baby last July, John said

it was a shame, my wasting water
in an apron—I could water crops
with all them tears. He grieved as well,
but what a thing. My mother used to say

we write our injuries in marble,
our kindnesses in dust.

Eugene Samples, pastor

Some say they come because the blowing ground
choked off their food. Others, that there aren't
enough coyotes left to keep them down.
Jackrabbits. Thousands. Eating every last

green thing. Back east, when I preached
the Bible's plagues, it was to illustrate
a spiritual event. But now—Lord,

it is made flesh. A "rabbit drive."
The whole town clubbing them to death.
The heaps of bodies piled up like hay.

I guess the Russians, who don't believe
in God, do worse. Today's the clearest day
in months—a sky of Heaven. But a fine

coating of earth covers my Bible,
like the first handful tossed in a new grave.

Margaret Tsosie, shepherd

Three men with rifles say
they're from the BIA,

say this land
is overgrazed, say we

keep too many
goats and sheep

for our size
reservation.

And that if we persist,
the plains will come down

on all our heads.
What happens next

we still have dreams about.
Children watching,

all of us screaming
stop, and when they do

it is to pour
gasoline over the bodies

of our dying
flocks and let them burn.

Then rot.
Persistence:

heaps of bones.
Blood on the cliff.

I didn't know I had
tears left.

Art MacAdams, fisherman

Sailing home from Georges Bank—a cloud
in a new shape. Blowing not rain

but dirt. Upside down, sky full of dirt, land
raining on the open sea. The whole boat,

our catch. No one spoke
but prayers. When we docked on Friday

my wife said it was the Great Plains
fell on us. I said you're nuts—

we were a hundred miles miles out to sea.
But the pictures of their farms—covered

in sand dunes ten feet high, like our cove
after a hurricane. They tore up too much earth,

that's all. I'm glad I fish. I take my cod,
the ocean closes right back up.

Lula Bowen, housewife and Sunday school teacher

I wrap old flour sacks around my children's faces
to keep it from their mouths, tell them to play
the Three Wise Men, crossing the desert

to give gifts to the Christ Child. These days the desert
is in the biscuits, on the pillowslips, in all our hair.
Carl says the white towns might get relief

from Washington, but in Nicodemus
only relief we'll get is prayer.
Well, then. To calm myself I say a psalm.

As for man, his days are as grass—and stop
to help my baby cough. My baby coughing,
and Paul and Beulah too, and outside noon

turns to midnight, and the cloud's a mile high—
for the wind passeth over it, and it is gone
but I left out a part, I back up: *for He knoweth our frame,*

He remembereth that we are dust
and I feel something in me cry out
Do not forget us Lord

let us be more to you than dust
                don't let us
                                blow away

Joe Martin, bartender

Some bigwig in Washington says
to let the Great Plains go, it's past repair.
Another says to pave it over, that
that will stop the storms. But he owns
an asphalt plant. Roosevelt says no,
he's sending men out here
to teach folks how to fix the soil.

I had a lush here once,
broke every bottle on that shelf
and smashed the whole mirror to bits.
I was a long time cleaning up and paying.
For my stock, and then for court—
I didn't win. Judge said I had no business
serving drunks. But he seemed fine
at first. Just another man
who wanted every glass half full.

Earl Owens, sharecropper

What now? I was born
here. I don't know

another way. I got kinfolk
in Chicago, true—two cousins,

who had jobs packing meat.
Had, I say. My neighbor read

the papers to me where it said
twelve million pounds of dirt

fell on Chicago. *This* dirt,
falling on James and Walter's heads!

I got three kids. And no land of my own.
A wife sick with cough and worrying.

Chicken in a pot. Hands
in a knot. The difference—

What we hoped for.
What we got.

Jesse Prather, farmer

A cough syrup of sugar with two drops
of kerosene helps only for a while.

Our graveyard's buried under drifts, so
we'll drive the bodies down to Hutchinson.

If a storm hits then, I don't know what
we'll do—last storm, a man went off

a road he couldn't see; they found him
later, suffocated in his car.

John Franks. He was my friend.
I know I should be feeling more

about all this. Our one-year-old
on Tuesday. My wife's mother Friday night.

Goddamn this ruthless wind. God
help me. Ruth was our daughter's name.

Azzie Morton, sixth grader

Foreclosed. A word like a door
grownups shut in your face
and hiss behind, their voices
fast as snakes. I guess they're fighting

about me, but I can't think what I've done.
When Pop comes out he says
the plough's gone anyway,
so why keep the farm. Besides,

in California, I'll get to have
an orange every day.
Ma looks up then. She asks if I recall
the wheat fields

before the hard times came.
I try to picture it. But all I see
is oranges. Suns on every tree,
and inside each one, rain,

sweet as candy. Then I quit it—
it makes my belly ache. The cow
ate busted thistles at the end.
That was last week.

Jennifer Smith-Ewing, museum curator

In the Dust Bowl Room, one day I spent
so long setting up a recreated shack
I felt I lived there. I couldn't shake the sense—
finally, driving home, I left my car
and waded through the lush rows
of a soybean field. Then I felt *here* again—
planted, my sandals wet with earth, mist falling
from the jetting sprinkler heads, my legs so cool.

These days our water comes from underground.
The aquifer's half gone, but we do have
twenty years before it's dry. I know—
I work around the past all day; yet in myself
I don't believe I'll die. The skin on my belly
is so soft. Such fertile land.

~III~

Graveside

As we throw flowers
down the mouth of earth

a bee rises and stings my girl
beside her eye. Now

two kinds of tears
and two deaths here:

the dying bee
a curled lantern
to light your way to dirt

and you—

is it return enough
to become

a breath of wind
across the buzzing garden

driving perfume
from the throat of

a belled flower in the dusk

When My Daughter Builds with Blocks

She starts with pastures for the animals to graze,
a landscape marked by oak rectangles
running the perimeter of her domain
like old stone walls. A dark blue
construction paper pool is placed
beside a gate she then knocks down,
while nearby two plastic sheep
crop handfuls of real grass (pulled
from the backyard, still green)
while a cow and a very small horse look on.

Her farmhouse sits by the pasture's eastern wall;
roofless, the sunlight streams inside to where a table
(small wooden block) stands draped with a white cloth
of toilet paper, on which a meal
has been carefully laid: tiny fried eggs,
bowl of bead oranges, a pie baked in a bottle cap.

And the people! No bigger than my (opposable) thumb—
some with their faces worn off, some bald; others
with homemade skirts held on by rubber bands.
Each one placed inside so carefully, each named,
all called into being by her hand.
So whenever I am able, I walk into her house and lie
down in the center of the world,
on the scrap of Kleenex rug, and gaze up at her sky.

Such Fertile Land

1. Janelle Stevens, home health aide, Oklahoma

It's far below our well the fractures split
the rock. The gas sucked up, the wasted
water spit back down—just like the kids
do the last slurp of Coke in their mouths,

in and out the straw. If there's a bit
of sweetness left, they'll find a way to taste it.
I scold or slap them on their heads,
but they keep on. That nasty gurgling sound.

When the ground begins to move, Corrine calls
Mom, it's doing it again! Just keep
both feet on the floor, I say, it's not shaking hard.

It's only rocking us. Though not to sleep.
Together we watch as a few more apples
thud down from the tree in our yard.

2. Consuelo Ramos Garza, farmworker, California

Our well is dry. The tap gave sand, then air.
An hour away, the almond trees and cattle
and fields of corn still drink up and thrive,
but in our *comunidad* we battle
the heat like dogs dumped out from passing cars.

Our bottled water's almost gone, so drive
your troubles somewhere else. We keep praying,
all day. *Señor, te suplicamos. Que llueva,*
que caiga del cielo, Padre, may it fall from the skies,
may your grace soak this dry earth, *la tierra* you gave us—

Another stray showed up last night. At first
he hung around the yard with those sad eyes,
triste como Jesús, then all night baying
as if he was in love. But it was thirst.

3. In an arroyo, western Nevada

When   shuttered buds   know
    each dropped leaf   breath
                          was swollen in flow
        a different kind of

folded in brightness   become
    whose splintered
                  turned from
      unshadowed heat   break

Then   your face
       these hills   daughter
Listen   ghosted song
   in our bones   this place
        endless as
  once was   now

A Word from Our Raindrop

twelve hundred wells · in one county · dry

ground crazed with cracks · we watch you · distorted

through thin-walled bottles · your ration · contracted

we too mourn when · your faucets spit · sand

we feel the thirst against · your throats · deciding

whether to give the dog away · drive the dog · somewhere

to the rescue center leave her · drive yourself · kids maybe

they have showers yet · the water can't be · drunk

we know all about it · this poison · we drink

from your bean fields · our universe of rivers · from your feedlots

we take it up · among ourselves · to exist

as a possibility · as potential · is all any of us do

turning away · dispersed · vanishing

to the empty clouds · to the dead trees · arms flung open

Pastoral at the March

Our whole world stomps between us,
her small hands tugging ours along
until she breaks for a billowing fabric sun
at the corner of 6th Avenue.

Watch me run she calls, just as she did
at the farm that day, her thin limbs
flashing as she flew
past the barn, past the flowers

alive with honeybees,
and down the best hill, ours for rolling
until we fell together into clover,
everything three and green,

sweet as breath and hair.
But here the air is full of signs,
each waving one more danger,
one more anger, one more shining *should*;

voices rise and chant, the long river
of bodies floods the avenue
and someone's painted, along the sides
of each gray building,

the rising water level, marked in blue.
Love, what have we done—
I want to seize her, spirit her away,
as if I could unmake her

in the face of what we've made.
As if we'd ever give up
that hour in the field that day,
her fingers stained with earth

slipping from ours to run ahead
so we would chase her,
her laugh a banner streaming behind her,

and we caught her
just before she disappeared

into a tunnel of trees.

On Not Listening

After being dragged thirty yards
with chains around her ankles, then pushed
by the bucket loader of a bulldozer
to a standing position, because if she can
be made to walk the last few steps
to the abattoir, she will be deemed
healthy enough to be eaten,
the dairy cow

shrinks herself down
to the size of a common dust mite
and drifts into the canal
of the ear of a woman
taking a nap on the sofa.
It is the one place no one
has thought to look for her.

Deeper in she floats,
toward the vibrating
membrane of the drum
where she is eaten
by a vanished tiger,
who got there first.

As the Days Turn Shorter

Leaves of the gnarled dogwood
fall the color of old blood,

of mulled wine drunk
around a bonfire the first night of winter.

The search for the perfect one
is over. You'll do, and you,

and you too—you there
beside the pile of unburned logs,

fists jammed
in your narrow pockets.

The Winter We Lost Antarctica

We fashioned a Christmas tree
from a dead branch we found after a storm,

splayed flat as fan coral, wide
as a drawing of the Tree of Life. We sank it

in a coffee can we filled with cement,
and painted each branch of its delicate spreading

a fire engine red; decorated its boughs
with origami storks and owls.

And on the longest night of the year
we gathered with our neighbors to sing songs,

and some of the children held candles aloft
and they sang "Silent Night," the song breaking

the silence it sings of to replace it
with something I don't know what to call,

especially now that part of it was
in the spaces between notes

the groaning of the ice,
a line of the music no one

had thought of singing before this,
a line that could not now be unsung.

The next morning I still heard it,
all five harmonic parts, when the sun

streamed across the snow
like the promise of spring, the promise

of a living God, the promise of anything
we were ever promised breaking up, sliding—

With the Floor Swept

With the floor swept
and the sky quiet

the only movement visible
between the two

is floating
from the stick of incense

burning in the temple

A silence carved
from the impossible

like a statue carved
from the face

of a cliff the face
of a man carved

into rock
In the absence

of wind
the spiral rises

We take
everything

we take everything down
yet not this

smoke

Footnote

In the wilderness
of desert he eats
locusts and honey

eats one by one
a plague of beaded eyes
hard shells

from whose louvered folds
wings lift

In the branches
a wild hive

alive with bodies
deep in the curves
of the combs

dark bee sap drips
into his tattered hands

his mouth
a flood of sweetness

the gold river swallowing
hard bits of carapace
whose soft innards
keep him

his urine so sweet
flies follow him

and when he squats
in the bushes

undigested wings
gleam in his soil
like flecks of mica

The Map

Since we are fools, we aren't sure
what it is we're holding.

One of us hangs it, framed, on the wall
and charges admission.

One of us folds it into a hat
and crowns himself king.

Some kind of game board?
Another country's paper money?

Meanwhile, there's a castle, whatever
that word means to you.

Dancing in the courtyard. A time
of feasting, peace. But even so:

within its most secret chamber
a lamp is burning.

The fuel?
A piece of paper.

But the destruction of the map
does not destroy the road

it indicated. Or the treasure.
Or the stars.

Sunflowers

I'm looking at a photograph of two people I love
standing in a group of sunflowers
taller than their heads.

Her face does not look like the face
of someone whose shitty childhood
could form the librettos for several grand operas,

as his does not look like the face
of a man who's just been diagnosed with cancer.
No, they look like people who have spent a day

on their knees in a garden,
who know the patience all soil will teach you.
Above them, the faces of the sunflowers

look the way things look
when they have been loved all their lives,
their petals unfurled in a halo whose peeled sunlight

is the color I would choose
if someone said, Find a shade for joy.

At Midnight

Awake and near. Your breathing—
I slip into you the way the deer

we saw at midnight
between the bodega

and the shuttered laundromat
so delicately crossed the street and slipped

into the chainlink park.
Noiselessly up the sandy slope,

to nudge a swing with the velvet of her mouth.
Sheltered by the stunted city trees

and the metal playground poles,
as I am sheltered in your body, not

what I'd have thought
when I thought *shelter,*

and yet our natures not so changed—
still her soft ears pricked

at the creak of chains in motion,
lifting her head from the swung pendulum

under small leaves bright in the streetlights
and green, love, green as any spring.

After This, Earth

could become a worry
stone in the pocket

of space, or a mood ring
on the finger of a newly minted

god. Perhaps a sucker
for a throat sore

from again and again
saying the same thing.

Or a locket at the neck
of an aurora—

inside, old photographs
of icebergs: the blue

cracking open
to sing.

Anthropocene Birthday

Gift of equations
    the empty orchard blossoming with snow

Gift of a haunting
    the shadows of the animals in smoke

Gift of a cinder
    the stars leapt from the bottom of the well

Gift of scar tissue
    the afterimage scored for us like notes

Gift of our silence
    so gently the sea covers up our words

Gift of a fever
    the smell of thunder breaking up the heat

Gift of a morning
    the votive candles going out like breath

Gift of our footsteps
    the leaves we saw caught in the hedge are birds

Acknowledgments

Grateful acknowledgment is made to the journals in which the following poems appeared, some in slightly different form:

Cimarron Review: "Deus ex Machina"
Hayden's Ferry Review: "Mobile"
Interim: "Graveside," "Poolside," "Such Fertile Land," "Study Guide"
Kudzu House: "When My Daughter Builds with Blocks"
The Nation: "Border"
New Delta Review: "Diner"
New Haven Review: "Pastoral," "Footnote"
Rattle: "Stalin," "A Story"
Spoon River Poetry Review: "Fire Burns Grass," "Phone Call After a Fire"
The Southern Review: "After This, Earth"

My sincere thanks to Marianne Boruch, Daisy Fried, Jennifer Givhan, Benjamin S. Grossberg, Cynthia Quiñones, Martha Rhodes, Clare Rossini, Mary Szybist, Lesley Valdes, and all the students and teachers I had the privilege of working with at Warren Wilson. Your keen attention, thoughtful critique, and unflagging encouragement guided every page of this collection.

I am grateful to the MFA Program for Writers at Warren Wilson College and the Sustainable Arts Foundation for their generous grants, including WWC's Barnhardt Scholarship.

Thank you to my dear friends and family, especially Vee and Cecilia: without your love and support, this book would not exist.

To all those courageously using their voices and their bodies to be the mouth of Earth, my deepest respect and gratitude. May we persist and endure.

Notes

"Dust": Homesteading Acts of the late nineteenth and early twentieth centuries encouraged white American settlers to establish farms and ranches on land from which Native American populations had been forcibly removed, including land on the Great Plains. A combination of over-ploughing, overgrazing of cattle, unscrupulous real estate practices, laissez-faire agricultural policy, and disregard for the inherent nature and capacity of the land all created the conditions for the Dust Bowl, a ten-year period of so-called "black blizzards" that nearly destroyed the Great Plains' ecosystem. The narrators of "Dust" and "Such Fertile Land" are invented personas, but the events they describe are factual:

> "*Eugene Samples*": The largest recorded "rabbit drive" occurred in Lane County, Kansas, when approximately ten thousand people clubbed thirty-five thousand jackrabbits to death in a single day.

> "*Margaret Tsosie*": The BIA is the Bureau of Indian Affairs, a federal agency. I based this poem's account of the slaughter of Native livestock by BIA officials on the witness testimony in *Dreaming of Sheep in Navajo County*, by anthropologist Marsha Weisiger.

> "*Art MacAdams*": This storm happened April 14, 1935.

> "*Lula Bowen*": In the fifty years following the Civil War, all-black towns and agricultural colonies were established on the Great Plains by African Americans fleeing ongoing persecution in the reconstructed South. More than fifty such towns and settlements existed in Oklahoma and Kansas; some, including Nicodemus, remain today.

> "*Earl Owens*": The "twelve million pounds of dirt dumped on Chicago" happened May 10–11, 1934.

"*Jennifer Smith-Ewing*": The Oglalla Aquifer lies beneath eight states of the Great Plains and is the source of approximately 30 percent of the ground water used for irrigation in the United States. Once the Oglalla is drained, it will take approximately six thousand years to recharge it with rainfall.

"*Janelle Stevens*": Since fracking began in Oklahoma, the annual number of earthquakes in the state that measure 3.0 or greater has jumped from fewer than 2 to 585. The Oklahoma Geological Survey has traced this increase to the underground disposal of contaminated water, a byproduct of fracking.

"*Consuelo Ramos Garza*": In 2015, 1,953 residential wells went dry in and around Tulare County, California, leaving many residents dependent on emergency water donations.

About the Author

SARAH P. STRONG is the author of a previous poetry collection, *Tour of the Breath Gallery,* and two novels, *The Fainting Room* and *Burning the Sea.* Their work has appeared widely, including in *The Nation, Poetry Daily, Rattle, Cimarron Review, The Southwest Review, The Southern Review, Verse Daily,* and *The Sun.* They teach creative writing at the University of Hartford and Central Connecticut State University, and have received grants from the Sustainable Arts Foundation and the Connecticut Council of the Arts. They live near New Haven, Connecticut, with their spouse and daughter.